ONE PLUS ONE

ONE PLUS ONE

8 sessions for building intimacy and commitment in our marriage

by David P. Seemuth

VICTOR BOOKS

A DIVISION OF SCRIPTURE PRESS PUBLICATIONS INC.
USA CANADA ENGLAND

Copyediting: Jane Vogel
Cover Design: Grace K. Chan Mallette
Cover Illustration: Frank McShane
Interior Illustrations: Al Hering
Recommended Dewey Decimal Classification: 301.402
Suggested Subject Heading: SMALL GROUPS

ISBN: 1-56476-415-X

1   2   3   4   5   6   7   8   9   10   Printing / Year   99   98   97   96   95

VICTOR BOOKS
A division of SP Publications, Inc.
Wheaton, Illinois 60187

CONTENTS

PURPOSE: To develop intimacy and commitment in our marriages.

INTRODUCTION

One Plus One is for couples who want to build intimacy and commitment in their marriages. An in-depth Leader's Guide is included at the back of the book with suggested time guidelines to help you structure your emphases in small group discussion. Each of the 8 sessions contains the following elements:

❑ **Getting Acquainted**—activities or selected readings to help you begin thinking and sharing from your life and experiences about the subject of the session. Use only those options that seem appropriate for your group.

❑ **Gaining Insight**—questions and in-depth Bible study to help you gain principles from Scripture for life-related application.

❑ **Growing By Doing**—an opportunity to practice the truth learned in the Gaining Insight section.

❑ **Going the Second Mile**—a personal enrichment section for you to do on your own.

❑ **Pocket Principles**—brief guidelines inserted in the Leader's Guide to help the Group Leader learn small group leadership skills as needed.

❑ **Session Objectives**—goals listed in the Leader's Guide that describe what should happen in the group by the end of the session.

IS THIS YOUR FIRST SMALL GROUP?

'smol grüp: A limited number of individuals assembled together having some unifying relationship.

Kris'chen 'smol grüp: 4–12 persons who meet together on a regular basis, over a determined period of time, for the shared purpose of pursuing biblical truth. They seek to mature in Christ and become equipped to serve as His ministers in the world.

Picture Your First Small Group.

List some words that describe what you want your small group to look like.

What Kind Of Small Group Do You Have?
People form all kinds of groups based on gender, age, marital status, and so forth. There are advantages and disadvantages to each. Here are just a few:

❑ **Same Age Groups** will probably share similar needs and interests.

❏ **Intergenerational Groups** bring together people with different perspectives and life experiences.

❏ **Men's or Women's Groups** usually allow greater freedom in sharing and deal with more focused topics.

❏ **Singles or Married Groups** determine their relationship emphases based on the needs of a particular marital status.

❏ **Mixed Gender Groups** (**singles and/or couples**) stimulate interaction and broaden viewpoints while reflecting varied lifestyles.

However, the most important area of "alikeness" to consider when forming a group is an **agreed-on purpose.** Differences in purpose will sabotage your group and keep its members from bonding. If, for example, Mark wants to pray but not play while Jan's goal is to learn through playing, then Mark and Jan's group will probably not go anywhere. People need different groups at different times in their lives. Some groups will focus on sharing and accountability, some on work projects or service, and others on worship. *Your small group must be made up of persons who have similar goals.*

How Big Should Your Small Group Be?
The **fewest** people to include would be **4.** Accountability will be high, but absenteeism may become a problem.

The **most** to include would be **12.** But you will need to subdivide regularly into groups of 3 or 4 if you want people to feel cared for and to have time for sharing.

How Long Should You Meet?
8 Weeks gives you a start toward becoming a close community, but doesn't overburden busy schedules. Count on needing three or four weeks to develop a significant trust level. The smaller the group, the more quickly trust develops.

Weekly Meetings will establish bonding at a good pace and allow for accountability. The least you can meet and still be an effective group is once a month. If you choose the latter, work at individual contact among group members between meetings.

You will need **75 minutes** to accomplish a quality meeting. The larger the size, the more time it takes to become a healthy group. Serving refreshments will add 20–30 minutes, and singing and/or prayer time, another 20–30 minutes. Your time duration may be determined by the time of day you meet and by the amount of energy members bring to the group. Better to start small and ask for more time when it is needed because of growth.

What Will Your Group Do?

To be effective, each small group meeting should include:

1. **Sharing**—You need to share who you are and what is happening in your life. This serves as a basis for relationship building and becomes a springboard for searching out scriptural truth.

2. **Scripture**—There must always be biblical input from the Lord to teach, rebuke, correct, and train in right living. Such material serves to move your group in the direction of maturity in Christ and protects from pooled ignorance and distorted introspection.

3. **Truth in practice**—It is vital to provide opportunities for *doing* the Word of God. Experiencing this within the group insures greater likelihood that insights gained will be utilized in everyday living.

Other elements your group may wish to add to these three are: a time of **worship**, **specific prayer** for group members, **shared projects**, a time to **socialize** and enjoy **refreshments**, and **recreation**.

ONE

Love Is an Action Verb

Weddings and Marriage

Weddings. They are performed in all kinds of settings with all kinds of people in all kinds of weather. Every wedding has its own story. Sometimes people faint. In some the best man drops the ring, in others the maid of honor comes an hour late. Candles won't light, or perhaps they light too well, igniting the silk flowers attached to them. Inevitably emotions are high, mothers are hyper, fathers become teary-eyed, and everyone is convinced the couple will live happily ever after.

Marriage. This is what weddings are all about. With all the attention given to the wedding day, one almost forgets the years that will follow. But God's concern is for steady, strong marriages, not picture-perfect wedding days. A society can be strong and healthy only when the marriage bond is held in honor.

GETTING ACQUAINTED

Your Wedding

Every wedding has its own story. What's yours? When were you married and where was the ceremony held?

Did anything unusual happen during your wedding?

What made the day particularly meaningful?

Where did you honeymoon? What were the high points and low points?

Your Marriage
What dreams did you have for your marriage when you said, "I do"?

What dreams do you have for your marriage now?

Love Is . . .
Which of the following popular statements about love best expresses your attitude when you were first married?

❑ "Love is blind."
❑ "Love is a many-splendored thing."
❑ "All you need is love."
❑ "Love makes the world go 'round."
❑ "Love conquers all."

In this session we will look at what love truly is.

14

GAINING INSIGHT

Love in Action

First Corinthians 13 is probably the most often read section of Scripture. We may find it easy to be lulled by the familiar words and to ignore the treasures there. But let's do our best to see God's plan to put love in action!

Read 1 Corinthians 13:1-7, 13.

¹If I speak in the tongues of men and of angels, but have not love, I am only a resounding gong or a clanging cymbal. ²If I have the gift of prophecy and can fathom all mysteries and all knowledge, and if I have a faith that can move mountains, but have not love, I am nothing. ³If I give all I possess to the poor and surrender my body to the flames, but have not love, I gain nothing. ⁴Love is patient, love is kind. It does not envy, it does not boast, it is not proud. ⁵It is not rude, it is not self-seeking, it is not easily angered, it keeps no record of wrongs. ⁶Love does not delight in evil but rejoices with the truth. ⁷It always protects, always trusts, always hopes, always perseveres.

¹³And now these three remain: faith, hope and love. But the greatest of these is love.

1 Corinthians 13:1-7, 13

The Apostle Paul writes this passage in the middle of a section on spiritual gifts. He is making the point that, no matter what kind of gift you personally have, and no matter how you may be using the gift, without love any gift is essentially worthless. This is especially true in marriage! We can be good at doing many things in our marriages, but without the attitude and actions of love, those abilities are meaningless.

Notice how Paul has identified several different actions and gifts that he hopes would be a part of the Christian's life. To make this passage come alive in the context of marriage, rewrite the first three verses to speak specifically to the husband/wife relationship. What are several things you can do in marriage that are meaningless without love?

My Loving Spouse
Identify instances when your spouse has demonstrated the characteristics and qualities of love.

Love is—

❏ Patient—My spouse needs patience when I . . .

❏ Kind—I have seen the kindness of my spouse when . . .

❏ Not boastful—I won't call attention to my own acts and accomplishments, but my spouse has these great qualities . . .

Partners with Power
Love is described in verse 4 as "not proud." In other words, lovers are to be humble and gentle. Each of us has tremendous power to heal and to hurt. Our power can be seen in the way we use our tongues, finances, time, and attitudes. We are to use our power as God would: for the well-being of others.

In what way have you seen the need to direct your power for the benefit of your spouse? List several ways you have used or would like to use your power for his or her benefit.

❏ Speech

❏ Money

❏ Time

❑ Attitudes

GROWING BY DOING

I Could Try This

Divide up the group so that men are meeting with men and women with women. Then discuss different ways you can put some of the words of the Apostle Paul into action in your life and marriage. Suggestions should be very specific, and they should be things you are able to accomplish in the next few weeks.

How can we men or women be more:

❑ Patient

❑ Kind

❑ Not self-seeking

❑ Open to our spouse's truthful comments

I'd Like You to Try That

Now pair up with your spouse. Take turns sharing the ideas you had. Ask your spouse which ideas seem especially to meet his or her needs, or would especially please him or her. Make those your priority!

17

GOING THE SECOND MILE

In My Life

Paul tells us that love does not keep a record of wrongs. Is there some incident or action for which you have not yet fully forgiven your spouse? If so, write it down and determine before God that this, indeed, will be the last time you hold your spouse guilty before you.

As a symbolic gesture of not keeping a record of this wrong, you might like to take a black marker and blot out what you have written. (It will also help you resist the temptation to leave this page open "accidentally" so your spouse can see his or her great wrong!)

For My Wife or Husband

Reflect on the actions your spouse highlighted in the **Growing by Doing** section. Which can you do this week? What will you do to actively show your love for your spouse?

For Our Group

Together with your husband or wife, pray for one couple from your small group. List their names and what you will pray about.

TWO

Choices

Hype or Hope?

Be proactive! Take charge of your life! You can do it if you put your mind to it! Be all that you can be! Ah, the slogans of life. Advertising executives are able to coin phrases to lead us. But these slogans, quickly adopted, just as quickly fade.

But advice that has stood the test of time is worth listening to. In the business world, W. Edwards Deming began to catch the attention of the greatest companies of the West because of his time-tested advice. Dr. Deming revolutionized Japanese industry after World War II and nearly single-handedly shaped the Japanese industrial world with his leadership and management methods. After his work became known in the United States, he became one of the most sought after business consultants. His advice was valuable because it was time-tested, enduring, proven.

In today's session we will examine the advice of a pioneer, someone who walked a path of effectiveness. Joshua was led by God to accomplish great things among all Israel. At the end of his life, he gave Israel advice for living. Such advice will help us in the long, exciting journey of marriage.

GETTING ACQUAINTED

Learning the Trail from Trailblazers
Joshua urged the Israelites to look back and see how God had rescued them from harm. In our marriages we have been given advice or have noticed role models who showed us the way. Who were those key people who provided the lead for you, either in word or in deed?

What help did you gain from these people? What advice or suggestions do you retain because of them?

How have you been able to incorporate these important lessons in your marriage?

Trail Map
If you were to map out the path your marriage has taken so far, what would it look like? Sketch a map in the space below, including any deserts, oases, mountain peaks, and valleys you would like to share with the group.

GAINING INSIGHT

Looking Back
Today we look at Joshua 24. At the end of his life, Joshua admonishes the people of Israel to make correct choices. Primary is the choice for families to single-mindedly serve

22

the Lord. Because of what God has done on Israel's behalf, serving God is a reasonable choice. But it is not automatic; they must choose. Then, as now, choices were linked to the past as well as to future directions.

Read Joshua 24:1-13.

¹Then Joshua assembled all the tribes of Israel at Shechem. He summoned the elders, leaders, judges and officials of Israel, and they presented themselves before God.

²Joshua said to all the people, "This is what the LORD, the God of Israel, says: 'Long ago your forefathers, including Terah the father of Abraham and Nahor, lived beyond the River and worshiped other gods. ³But I took your father Abraham from the land beyond the River and led him throughout Canaan and gave him many descendants. I gave him Isaac, ⁴and to Isaac I gave Jacob and Esau. I assigned the hill country of Seir to Esau, but Jacob and his sons went down to Egypt.

⁵" 'Then I sent Moses and Aaron, and I afflicted the Egyptians by what I did there, and I brought you out. ⁶When I brought your fathers out of Egypt, you came to the sea, and the Egyptians pursued them with chariots and horsemen as far as the Red Sea. ⁷But they cried to the LORD for help, and He put darkness between you and the Egyptians; He brought the sea over them and covered them. You saw with your own eyes what I did to the Egyptians. Then you lived in the desert for a long time.

⁸" 'I brought you to the land of the Amorites who lived east of the Jordan. They fought against you, but I gave them into your hands. I destroyed them from before you, and you took possession of their land. ⁹When Balak son of Zippor, the king of Moab, prepared to fight against Israel, he sent for Balaam son of Beor to put a curse on you. ¹⁰But I would not listen to Balaam, so he blessed you again and again, and I delivered you out of his hand.

¹¹" 'Then you crossed the Jordan and came to Jericho. The citizens of Jericho fought against you, as did also the Am-

orites, Perizzites, Canaanites, Hittites, Girgashites, Hivites and Jebusites, but I gave them into your hands. ¹²I sent the hornet ahead of you, which drove them out before you — also the two Amorite kings. You did not do it with your own sword and bow. ¹³So I gave you a land on which you did not toil and cities you did not build; and you live in them and eat from vineyards and olive groves that you did not plant.'

Joshua 24:1-13

Joshua begins his remarks to the key people of Israel by recounting what God had said to the nation. He will have further comments, surely, but his focus is first of all on God's Word. In order to get Joshua's message, summarize the following sections from God's message to Israel:

❑ Joshua 24:2-4

❑ Joshua 24:5-7

❑ Joshua 24:11-13

What theme comes through loud and clear in the verses you just summarized?

How have you experienced that theme in your life? If Joshua were recounting God's faithfulness to you personally, what would he say in his speech?

How does this section prepare the people to hear God's commands?

How does God's work in your life prepare you to hear His commands?

Time to Choose
Next Joshua gives three commands (actually four, but one is repeated). Read Joshua 24:14 and list those commands:

¹⁴**"Now fear the LORD and serve Him with all faithfulness. Throw away the gods your forefathers worshiped beyond the River and in Egypt, and serve the LORD.**
Joshua 24:14

Commands:

1.

2.

3.

Most of us will not have served other gods in the sense of deities from other lands. We are, however, tempted to follow other things in place of God. We, too, are idolatrous.

What are the most difficult temptations we have to serve other "gods" in our present modern age?

How does our society encourage this kind of idolatry?

What impact might this kind of idolatry have on our marriages?

Notice how Joshua puts the choice plainly before the people.

¹⁵But if serving the LORD seems undesirable to you, then choose for yourselves this day whom you will serve, whether the gods your forefathers served beyond the River, or the gods of the Amorites, in whose land you are living. But as for me and my household, we will serve the LORD."

Joshua 24:15

Remember, these people have been with Joshua for many years. They are part of the covenant people Israel. One might think that they have already made and demonstrated their decision. But at this turning point in Israel's history, Joshua places a clear challenge to these elders, leaders, and officials.

At what crucial points in a marriage or in family life might we need to reaffirm our commitment to God?

 ## GROWING BY DOING

As for Me . . .
To what extent have you, personally, made a decision to follow the Lord? What has your spiritual journey been like? What are the significant points along the way?

And My Household
Form groups of two or three couples (keeping husbands and wives together) and discuss the following questions.

❏ What has serving the Lord as a couple or family meant in your marriage so far? What are some specific ways you have served the Lord as a couple or family?

❏ How does a commitment to serve God affect a marriage?

❏ What are specific ways we can serve God as couples or families right now?

Commitment to God is vital for a healthy marriage. But Christian couples often complain of "overcommitment" to church causes, committees, and activities—an overload that hinders rather than enhances marital and family life.

❏ How can we balance active service with the need for time to spend with spouse and family?

GOING THE SECOND MILE

In My Life
What kinds of steps can you take which will help you to confirm a decision (or perhaps step closer to a decision) to serve the Lord and to yield your heart to the Lord? What is standing in your way?

For My Wife or Husband
Ask your wife or husband how you can be encouraging in his or her spiritual journey. What can you do to help? How will you help this week?

For Our Group
As a couple, pray for your prayer partner couple in the group. Can you support them in any tangible way as they serve God?

THREE

Can We Talk?

Sticks and Stones May Break My Bones . . .
Physical tools of destruction seldom inflict the deepest wounds. Words, with no material essence, tear into people, causing pain that sometimes lasts a lifetime. But words can also heal, help, and set free. "The tongue of the wise brings healing," Proverbs 12:18 declares. But let people cut us off on the road, and we respond with words that hardly will balm their hurting hearts!

Such aggravation isn't only limited to road experiences. Two people living in close proximity are bound to "cut off" each other in daily life. And sometimes angry words fly. On the other hand, we also know that words spoken with depth of feeling and love can lift marriage partners up from the pit of despair. Tender words light the fire of passionate love. Isn't that what we desire in our marriages? "But," you may respond, "that is not my experience in my marriage." That may be true. Whether it is true or not, we all agree we can strive to be better in our communication patterns.

God has given us guidance through the Scriptures for speaking to one another in love. So when your spouse asks, "Can we talk?" not only will you eagerly say, "Yes," but you will have the right tools to communicate effectively.

GETTING ACQUAINTED

Road Warriors
Complete the following sentences.

When other drivers annoy me on the road, I tend to respond by . . .

❑ graciously giving them the right of way.
❑ gently but firmly asserting my rights to the road.
❑ expanding my vocabulary in dubious ways.
❑ blowing my horn—just to be sure it works.
❑ making gestures I'd prefer not to demonstrate here.

When people annoy me in other areas of my life, I tend to respond by . . .

❑ graciously giving them the right of way.
❑ gently but firmly asserting my rights to the road.
❑ expanding my vocabulary in dubious ways.
❑ blowing my top.
❑ making gestures I'd prefer not to demonstrate here.

Old and New
Think of a time in your childhood when you received some desperately desired new object. What was it? How did you treat your new treasure once you had it?

Think of a new possession—clothes? a car?—that you received or acquired in the last year. What was it? Have you kept it "good as new" or has it already suffered the dents and dings of daily life?

In the passage we'll look at today, the Apostle Paul talks about the "old self"—that which does not know God—and the "new self"—that which is created to be like God (Ephesians 4:22-23). How did you feel when you first came to know God, or first realized what your faith could mean in your life?

What aspects of daily living threaten to prematurely age your "new self"?

GAINING INSIGHT

Putting Off the Old

The beloved Apostle Paul will give us very specific insights into the way we should communicate with others. Obviously, Paul has the church at large in view, not only married couples. But we certainly will learn from these principles to put godly patterns into our lives. And this enhances our marriages.

Read Ephesians 4:20-32.

²⁰You, however, did not come to know Christ that way. ²¹Surely you heard of Him and were taught in Him in accordance with the truth that is in Jesus. ²²You were taught, with regard to your former way of life, to put off your old self, which is being corrupted by its deceitful desires; ²³to be made new in the attitude of your minds; ²⁴and to put on the new self, created to be like God in true righteousness and holiness.

²⁵Therefore each of you must put off falsehood and speak truthfully to his neighbor, for we are all members of one body. ²⁶"In your anger do not sin": Do not let the sun go down while you are still angry, ²⁷and do not give the devil a foothold. ²⁸He who has been stealing must steal no longer, but must work, doing something useful with his own hands, that he may have something to share with those in need.

²⁹Do not let any unwholesome talk come out of your mouths, but only what is helpful for building others up according to their needs, that it may benefit those who listen. ³⁰And do not grieve the Holy Spirit of God, with whom you were sealed for the day of redemption. ³¹Get rid of all bitterness, rage and anger, brawling and slander, along with every form of malice. ³²Be kind and compas-

31

sionate to one another, forgiving each other, just as in Christ God forgave you.

Ephesians 4:20-32

In verses 20-24, Paul characterizes the "old self" and the "new self." How does Paul describe both?

❏ Old Self:

❏ New Self:

Paul speaks of putting off the old self with all of the destructive behaviors that go along with our old way of life. As you think about your communication patterns, what are the words and behaviors that could tend to "shut down" true, open, honest communication? Can you think of any examples of how they might appear in marriages?

Why do we tend to get locked in such patterns when we know they are not helpful?

Which of these do you see in your own communication style? Do you, personally, have any tendencies in this area?

Speech Class
Notice how Paul describes the Ephesians as being members of "one body" (4:25). This is obviously true of the church. It is even a more apt description of a married couple. What are the twin commands of Ephesians 4:25?
1.

2.

These two commands are not synonymous. In what way is it possible to obey one and not the other? Give examples.

What principle comes through in Ephesians 4:26-27? Do you think this is to be understood literally? Why or why not?

Have you applied this principle in your marriage? If you have, with what results?

In what way does holding a grudge against a spouse "give the devil a foothold"?

If we allow our anger to go unexpressed and bury it, what will happen to the relationship with the other person? Have you ever seen this happen in a marriage? When have you seen it and how can you learn from this example?

It is usually the people closest to us that seem to be the targets of our anger. Paul gives some specific commands on dealing with behaviors that may hurt our relationships with others. Give examples that might occur in marriage.

❏ "Do not let any unwholesome talk come out of your mouths" (v. 29)

❏ Speak "only what is helpful for building others up according to their needs." (v. 29)

33

❏ "Get rid of all bitterness . . . slander . . . " (v. 31)

Paul does not neglect the positive. He notes the importance of actions that are modeled by Christ Himself. Note the admonitions in Ephesians 4:32.

❏ Be . . .

❏ Be . . .

❏ Be . . .

GROWING BY DOING

Kind and Compassionate
Divide into groups of men and women. Make a list of kind and compassionate acts you could do for your spouse. This can be a brainstorm session with others who will help you if you need other ideas. In this way you can consciously "put off the old self" and "put on the new self."

What kind and compassionate acts would you like your spouse to do for you? Use your communication skills to list them in a positive—not a complaining—style!

GOING THE SECOND MILE

In My Life

Are you aware of any areas in which you are harboring bitterness in your heart against your spouse? If so, how can you resolve them?

Is your spouse giving you signals that he or she has something against you? How can you take steps to address these things?

For My Wife or Husband

Ask your wife or husband which of the compassionate and kind ideas you listed in **Growing by Doing** she or he would most appreciate. List them below. Which can you do this week?

For Our Group

As a couple, think of at least one kind or compassionate act you could do for your prayer-partner couple in the group. Carry through on it!

FOUR

Recipe for Maximum Enjoyment

Half-baked or Heavenly?

We all have our favorite dishes prepared in ways that seem especially pleasing to us. Chocolate chip cookie connoisseurs know exactly the way they like their cookies. Some like them soft, others crunchy. Some prefer pecans, others insist on macadamia nuts. When we find a recipe that fits our exact requirements, we stick with it.

Marriages are mixed to a variety of recipes, as well. But what do we do when a pecan lover marries a macadamia aficionado? Too often, as we try to exact our own personal enjoyment out of marriage, one feels used and the other feels selfish. This is not God's way for marriage. What we need is a recipe from God for fulfillment in marriage.

 GETTING ACQUAINTED

Just Desserts

What is your favorite dessert?

Who prepares it the best?

What makes this recipe better than others?

Choice Ingredients
Who, in your opinion, has an honorable marriage, one that is marked by mutual fulfillment?

Why does this couple seem to have such a good relationship? What "ingredients" do they use in their marriage?

Which of these "ingredients" do you long to perfect in your marriage? Why?

GAINING INSIGHT

Living Wisely
The Apostle Paul wrote about living wisely in our key relationships. In looking at his commands, we gain a recipe for fulfillment in marriage.

Read Ephesians 5:15-33.

Be very careful, then, how you live — not as unwise but as wise, ¹⁶making the most of every opportunity, because the days are evil. ¹⁷Therefore do not be foolish, but understand what the Lord's will is. ¹⁸Do not get drunk on wine, which leads to debauchery. Instead, be filled with the Spirit. ¹⁹Speak to one another with psalms, hymns and spiritual songs. Sing and make music in your heart to the Lord, ²⁰always giving thanks to God the Father for everything, in the name of our Lord Jesus Christ.

²¹**Submit to one another out of reverence for Christ.**

²²**Wives, submit to your husbands as to the Lord. ²³For the husband is the head of the wife as Christ is the head of the church, His body, of which He is the Savior. ²⁴Now as the church submits to Christ, so also wives should submit to their husbands in everything.**

²⁵**Husbands, love your wives, just as Christ loved the church and gave Himself up for her ²⁶to make her holy, cleansing her by the washing with water through the Word, ²⁷and to present her to Himself as a radiant church, without stain or wrinkle or any other blemish, but holy and blameless. ²⁸In this same way, husbands ought to love their wives as their own bodies. He who loves his wife loves himself. ²⁹After all, no one ever hated his own body, but he feeds and cares for it, just as Christ does the church — ³⁰for we are members of His body. ³¹"For this reason a man will leave his father and mother and be united to his wife, and the two will become one flesh." ³²This is a profound mystery — but I am talking about Christ and the church. ³³However, each one of you also must love his wife as he loves himself, and the wife must respect her husband.**

Ephesians 5:15-33

General Guidelines

Many people turn to Ephesians 5:22-33 for specific guidelines for marriage. While this section certainly contains much to look at, we must not remove these verses from their immediate context. Paul sets up his advice on marriage with commands on how to live in general in relationships. In Ephesians 5:15-21, Paul provides the foundation for what he is to say later.

Notice the command to "be careful how you live" (Ephesians 5:15). Following this admonition are three couplets. First Paul states what we should not do; then he says what we should do. What are these couplets?

❏ Ephesians 5:15b   Not . . .
                            But . . .

❏ Ephesians 5:17   Not . . .
                            But . . .

❏ Ephesians 5:18   Not . . .
                            But . . .

Paul goes on to describe what behaviors flow from a life controlled by the Spirit. What are these behaviors, according to Ephesians 5:19-21?

Practically speaking, how can we incorporate these behaviors into everyday life? How do they look in a twentieth-century context?

Guidelines for Marriage
Paul concludes his general guidelines with an exhortation to mutual submission (v. 21). He then describes what this looks like. What are the key statements for husbands and wives in Ephesians 5:22-33?

❏ Wives:

❏ Husbands:

A wife's submission to her husband is in the context of his own submission to her and in the fullness of a spirit-filled life. The wife is to do this voluntarily and must not be commanded to do it by the husband. It is her free choice.

What might voluntary submission to a husband look like?

What do you think would be an abuse of this command?

Notice the kind of husband a wife is submitting to. The way of the husband is to be the way of Christ.

What is the manner of Jesus, and how does this apply to marriage?

What does this kind of love do to our understanding of the command to mutually submit?

GROWING BY DOING

Submission Scenarios

On separate slips of paper, have each group member describe a conflict that could arise in marriage. As couples, take turns drawing a slip and role playing how a couple acting in mutual submission might deal with that conflict.

After each role play, discuss as a group:

- ❏ Was this a realistic solution? Why or why not?
- ❏ Would you be comfortable with this solution if you were the wife? If you were the husband?
- ❏ Would this solution work in your marriage? Why or why not?
- ❏ What other ways might you approach this conflict?

The Spirit-filled Marriage

Discuss with your own spouse the following:

What can be done in your lives to facilitate the life of spiritual fullness?

Since one of Paul's commands deals with giving thanks, compile a list of things for which you as a couple are thankful.

What can you as a couple do this week that will be a step toward having a spirit-filled marriage?

GOING THE SECOND MILE

In My Life

What are areas of your life are lived in an unwise fashion? How will you personally take steps to lead a life in the fullness of the Spirit in line with God's will?

For My Wife or Husband

Initiate a prayer time with your spouse that focuses on thanksgiving.

For Our Group

Prepare a statement that expresses how your life is different because of putting these principles into practice. What has happened to your attitude in so doing? How has your spouse responded? Take the statement to the next session to share.

FIVE

One Plus One Equals One

Strange Mathematics

A sex-crazed society. A people with an overriding concern for things of the flesh. Prostitution common in the cities. Perverse sexual expression seemingly ever-present, almost celebrated. Does this describe the twentieth century? Perhaps. But it also described the first century, the century in which Paul lived. Paul's concern was to address the people of God about how God intends us to behave sexually.

Few would deny the importance of sexual expression in marriage. The sexual realm is the honored, celebrated gift of God for marriage. Sexual union is intended to provide closeness not found in other relationships. But we sometimes shy away from talking about the subject. Much of the "celebration" of the pleasure of sex comes from those who do not use it as God intended.

So, let's look at the subject in a way that honors God and celebrates the joy God intended for married couples. Two individuals coming together in sexual union "become one." This is truly a remarkable event. One plus one actually equals one.

GETTING ACQUAINTED

A Great Idea!
Describe your favorite romantic setting. If you were to plan a romantic time with your spouse, what would you include?

What factors hinder you from carrying out these ideas?

What makes the romantic event so special in your mind?

Sex and Romance
How would you describe the relationship between sex and romance? How do you think your spouse would describe it?

It has been said that women value romance more than sex and men value sex more than romance. Do you agree? Explain.

GAINING INSIGHT

Sex for Christians
Paul is so intensely practical. He understood the dynamics that are at work in individuals and couples. He also understood his society, which seemed to work against sexual purity and which cheapened sexual expression. But most of all Paul understood God's intention for sex. It is something grand, reserved for the married couple.

Read 1 Corinthians 6:16–7:5.

¹⁶Do you not know that he who unites himself with a prostitute is one with her in body? For it is said, "The two will become one flesh." ¹⁷But he who unites himself with the Lord is one with Him in spirit.

¹⁸Flee from sexual immorality. All other sins a man commits are outside his body, but he who sins sexually sins against his own body. ¹⁹Do you not know that your body is a temple of the Holy Spirit, who is in you, whom you have received from God? You are not your own; ²⁰you were bought at a price. Therefore honor God with your body.

¹Now for the matters you wrote about: It is good for a man not to marry. ²But since there is so much immorality, each man should have his own wife, and each woman her own husband. ³The husband should fulfill his marital duty to his wife, and likewise the wife to her husband. ⁴The wife's body does not belong to her alone but also to her husband. In the same way, the husband's body does not belong to him alone but also to his wife. ⁵Do not deprive each other except by mutual consent and for a time, so that you may devote yourselves to prayer. Then come together again so that Satan will not tempt you because of your lack of self-control.

1 Corinthians 6:16–7:5

Paul is very aware of the power of sex. Used in the proper context, sex is a wonderful gift. Used wrongly, it is a horrible sin. This section of First Corinthians provides both "do's" and "don'ts" about sex. We will look at both to understand both the proper expression of sex and its misuse.

Sex outside Marriage

Based on this passage, how would you respond to a person who says, "I feel that my sexual behavior has nothing to do with my religion, because sex is physical and religion is spiritual"?

Do you think that this passage demonstrates that sexual sin is worse than other kinds of sin? Why or why not?

How does the fact that you were bought at a price (6:20) motivate you?

Sex within Marriage
Sex as a duty (7:3) is not a popular concept. In what ways do husbands and wives have responsibilities to each other sexually? What are the benefits to the spouse of fulfilling those responsibilities? What are the benefits to the marriage?

What obstacles might prevent couples from fulfilling their responsibilities to each other?

How do you feel about your body not belonging to you alone? (7:4)

How does this perspective run counter to society's attitudes?

How might the idea of a person's body belonging to his or her spouse be abused?

How could the idea be honored in a way that is truly pleasing to God and to the spouse?

Paul suggests that sexual intimacy in marriage is a defense against temptation (7:5). In what ways is this the case?

GROWING BY DOING

Supporting One Another
In what ways does our society tempt us to be unfaithful in our sexual lives? What situations can leave us particularly vulnerable?

How can Christians support one another in sexual purity? What can we do as members of this group to support one another?

Who's Got the Time/Energy/Privacy . . . ?
Divide into two groups, men with men and women with women. In your same-sex group, list stresses, distractions, and obstacles to making sexual intimacy a priority in marriage.

Now listen to the other group and jot down their comments here.

What can you do to alleviate some of the stresses and distractions your spouse faces?

GOING THE SECOND MILE

In My Life
Are there any areas which are not honoring to God in your sexual life? How can you make these right? What can you do to honor God and your partner in this crucial area?

Write down your thoughts regarding your sexual life. Which aspects of it are very rewarding? Which areas need work? What are some of the barriers that hinder full expression in this area?

For My Wife or Husband
Plan a time when you can talk to your spouse about what you can do to make your sexual life more rewarding. Write down when and where you will discuss this.

Plan a romantic date with your spouse. Carry it out this week, if possible!

For Our Group
Write a prayer for your group which will express your concern for holiness in the area of sex. Pray that there might be purity and fulfillment for others.

SIX

Money — Yours, Mine, and Ours

Budget Blues
The one conclusion that most people can agree about concerning money is that we don't have enough of it. As a result, we scurry around to see if we can acquire more and more. In order to make sure we are not keeping it, advertisers spend enormous amounts of time, effort, and, yes, money to see that we send some of our money their way. In so doing, we create a deficit that pushes us to stay on the treadmill of acquisition. Eventually, if we don't keep up with the pace, we either declare bankruptcy, find another job, or try to live within our means.

Financial matters are too often a source of conflict within marriage. Very few couples seem to have more money than days left at the end of a month. So we must learn the lessons of contentment and perspective. Perhaps we need to learn management as well. But for sure we must look at the Scriptures to learn God's perspective on this vital issue.

 GETTING ACQUAINTED

Your First Purchase
What was your first major purchase you remember (something you saved up for for a long time)? Why did you want it?

What were your feelings and thoughts when you finally acquired it?

What role does that item have in your life now? If you don't have it, what happened to it?

What is your most treasured possession now?

GAINING INSIGHT

True Treasure

Jesus addressed the disciples and the crowds about things that should gain our true attention. He also warned against spiritual dangers. In this session we'll look at Jesus' admonitions regarding possessions. Jesus is confronted first of all by a person desiring what he considers belongs to him: an inheritance. Jesus answers with a parable and then uses the incident to teach the disciples about priorities regarding material things. Let us listen in, as it were, as Jesus' disciples hear Him.

Read Luke 12:13-34.

¹³Someone in the crowd said to Him, "Teacher, tell my brother to divide the inheritance with me."

¹⁴Jesus replied, "Man, who appointed Me a judge or an arbiter between you?" ¹⁵Then He said to them, "Watch out! Be on your guard against all kinds of greed; a man's life does not consist in the abundance of his possessions."

¹⁶And He told them this parable: "The ground of a certain rich man produced a good crop. ¹⁷He thought to himself, 'What shall I do? I have no place to store my crops.'

¹⁸"Then he said, 'This is what I'll do. I will tear down my barns and build bigger ones, and there I will store all my

grain and my goods. ¹⁹And I'll say to myself, 'You have plenty of good things laid up for many years. Take life easy; eat, drink and be merry.'

²⁰"But God said to him, 'You fool! This very night your life will be demanded from you. Then who will get what you have prepared for yourself?'

²¹"This is how it will be with anyone who stores up things for himself but is not rich toward God."

²²Then Jesus said to His disciples: "Therefore I tell you, do not worry about your life, what you will eat; or about your body, what you will wear. ²³Life is more than food, and the body more than clothes. ²⁴Consider the ravens: They do not sow or reap, they have no storeroom or barn; yet God feeds them. And how much more valuable you are than birds! ²⁵Who of you by worrying can add a single hour to his life? ²⁶Since you cannot do this very little thing, why do you worry about the rest?

²⁷"Consider how the lilies grow. They do not labor or spin. Yet I tell you, not even Solomon in all his splendor was dressed like one of these. ²⁸If that is how God clothes the grass of the field, which is here today, and tomorrow is thrown into the fire, how much more will He clothe you, O you of little faith! ²⁹And do not set your heart on what you will eat or drink; do not worry about it. ³⁰For the pagan world runs after all such things, and your Father knows that you need them. ³¹But seek His kingdom, and these things will be given to you as well.

³²"Do not be afraid, little flock, for your Father has been pleased to give you the kingdom. ³³Sell your possessions and give to the poor. Provide purses for yourselves that will not wear out, a treasure in heaven that will not be exhausted, where no thief comes near and no moth destroys. ³⁴For where your treasure is, there your heart will be also."

Luke 12:13-34

Jesus' teachings here are crucial for our age. The advertising community is counting on the fact that most people will ignore the essence of Jesus' words. You will not find commercials saying, "We know you don't really need this stuff, but buy it anyway!" They convince us we must have it. Even in families, when inheritances are divided, bitterness is often the result. Instead of the passing of a loved one being a time to unite a family, it divides. Greed creeps in; self-centeredness wins.

Jesus' teachings fall into two natural units. Summarize each section as indicated below:

❏ Luke 12:13-21

❏ Luke 12:22-34

Let's look at these sections one by one.

Rich Fools
Jesus is approached as a rabbi. Rabbis often settled legal disputes. A man wants to lure Jesus into making a decision about legal matters. Jesus refuses. Instead, He warns against greed. The man must have been quite put off. But Jesus focuses on spiritual issues as most important. When these spiritual principles are properly applied, the material issues also come into proper focus.

What kind of forces work against us applying the truth of Luke 12:15?

Practically speaking, how does one guard against greed?

If a man's (or woman's) life does not consist in the abundance of his possessions (v. 15), of what does it consist? On what do you place value?

How do we balance what Jesus teaches in the parable with our responsibility to prepare for the future?

Why Worry?

How would you answer the questions Jesus asks in Luke 12:25-26?

On a scale of 1 (non-worrier) to 10 (major worrier), how would you rate yourself? How would you rate your husband?

How do the differences or similarities between your worry ratings affect how you handle money as a couple?

What kind of things "will be given to you" according to Luke 12:31? Why do we have trouble believing this?

How can you apply the principles of Jesus' words in verses 22-34? Be practical: how could Jesus' teaching affect the way you budget your time, your money, and your attentions? How would this affect your marriage?

GROWING BY DOING

Tough Truth

Which of the following statements do you most wrestle with in living a faith-oriented life? Why? Discuss in the group how to attack these issues.

☐ "A man's life does not consist in the abundance of his possessions" (Luke 12:15).

☐ "Do not worry about your life, what you will eat" (Luke 12:22).

☐ "Provide purses for yourselves that will not wear out, a treasure in heaven that will not be exhausted" (Luke 12:33).

GOING THE SECOND MILE

In My Life

How will you attack the attitudes that go against Jesus' teachings? Whom will you trust to challenge you in these areas?

For My Wife or Husband

What decisions have you made as a family that have gone against the spirit of these teachings? Which decisions have been good? How can you change what needs to be changed and enhance and encourage good decisions that are in line with Jesus' words?

For Our Group

Developing openness in the group is crucial to good group life. Could you share something about your attempts to put Jesus' teaching into your own marriage the next time you meet that will show how you are trying to be responsive to God's Word? What would you say? Will you say it?

SEVEN

Living a Life Daily

Same Old Same Old
"What's new?"

"Not much, I guess. What about with you?"

"Things are pretty much the same. Work is busy. I never seem to get enough time with my family. You know, the same old things."

Does this sound like a typical conversation? When we really get down to living, life is pretty much routine. We get up, take a shower, eat breakfast, get the kids off to school, go to work, eat lunch, work, come home, play with the kids, eat, get the kids to bed, collapse, and wait for the next day.

In the daily grind we must be careful not to ignore our key relationships. These tend to get lost simply in living. Fortunately, as disciples of Christ we need not be lost in the mundane. We can focus on God's plan to maintain good relationships and responsibly live in all spheres of life.

GETTING ACQUAINTED

A Daily Life

Fill in a calendar page showing how you spend a typical weekday.

Any Weekday

6:00 A.M.

8:00 A.M.

10:00 A.M.

12:00 A.M.

2:00 P.M

4:00 P.M.

6:00 P.M.

8:00 P.M.

10:00 P.M.

12:00 midnight

How do you view your life right now? Do you eagerly anticipate each day? Are you discouraged by the mundane aspects of life? What are the high and low points of your life?

What is a difficult aspect of your life right now? To what extent is this related to the "daily-ness" of life?

How does this impact your marriage?

GAINING INSIGHT

More than a Grind

Life was meant to be lived in relationship. In relationship with God, with family, with our spouses, and with others. But many men and women, even those who are married, testify to feeling desperately alone. The stresses of contemporary life isolate us even though our appointment books are full. Our study in this session will focus on living in relationship even in a life defined by "daily grinds."

Read Galatians 6:1-10.

¹**Brothers, if someone is caught in a sin, you who are spiritual should restore him gently. But watch yourself, or you also may be tempted. ²Carry each other's burdens, and in this way you will fulfill the law of Christ. ³If anyone thinks he is something when he is nothing, he deceives himself. ⁴Each one should test his own actions. Then he can take pride in himself, without comparing himself to somebody else, ⁵for each one should carry his own load.**

⁶**Anyone who receives instruction in the Word must share all good things with his instructor.**

⁷**Do not be deceived: God cannot be mocked. A man reaps what he sows. ⁸The one who sows to please his sinful nature, from that nature will reap destruction; the one who sows to please the Spirit, from the Spirit will reap eternal life. ⁹Let us not become weary in doing good, for at the proper time we will reap a harvest if we do not give up. ¹⁰Therefore, as we have opportunity, let us do good to all people, especially to those who belong to the family of believers.**

Galatians 6:1-12

Paul is concerned about sinning, sharing, and sowing. As we look at this section we will focus on each of these topics. We might think of these as warnings and orders to handle life's daily issues.

Concerning Sinning
How would one carry out the command given in Galatians 6:1?

What makes this a difficult task?

Have you been in a situation in which you were able to help restore someone after a sin? Or have you experienced such restoration yourself? If you can share the experience without betraying other people's confidences, do so.

How should we "watch" ourselves (v. 1) to not be tempted?

What are some typical, everyday situations that could give rise to temptation?

In what situations might marriage partners be especially equipped to "restore" one another? In what situations might it be easier to give or receive help from someone other than your spouse?

Concerning Sharing
What is the link between the command of Galatians 6:2 and the caution of Galatians 6:3?

How do we carry out the task of carrying one another's burdens? Share specific examples from your own experience, either as one who carried or one who was helped.

How does this command relate to carrying our own loads? (v. 5)

How do verses 2-5 apply to marriage? Give specific examples.

Concerning Sowing
Rephrase the spiritual principle described in Galatians 6:7 in your own words.

How can we sow properly, according to verses 8-9?

What does this mean in everyday life?

What does it mean in marriage?

 GROWING BY DOING

Bearing One Another's Burdens
A small group is an ideal place for the sharing of burdens. We all have needs that are greater than ourselves. These are things we need to unload, at least partially, onto others.

Part of helping others carry their burdens involves prayer. Divide into groups of four, and share with one another things that demand prayer. Do members of your foursome also have practical needs that can be lessened? List the name of each person, the prayer request, and other needs that can be met practically.

❑ Name:

❑ Name:

❑ Name:

❑ My own burden:

GOING THE SECOND MILE

In My Life
To what extent are you sowing the things that please the Spirit of God? Are there also areas where you are sowing to please the sinful nature? How will you grow the healthy harvest and weed out the harmful harvest?

For My Wife or Husband
Ask your spouse how you may be more effective in bearing his or her burdens. Find out specific needs for prayer and action.

For Our Group
As a couple, continue to pray for the needs mentioned during the **Growing by Doing** section. Can you act to help meet any of the needs mentioned?

EIGHT

Strength Enough to Finish

Secrets to Success

Every now and then we hear about couples who have been married fifty, sixty, or even seventy-five years. Reporters ask the secret to long, happy marriages. It takes a lot of grace to live that long with another person and have a relationship that continues to grow and thrive.

It also takes a proper attitude towards the future and the time we have remaining. It takes perseverance. This is true in all of life. In our concluding session, let's look at the principles for hanging in there until the end. Finishing well is the focus. We want to finish well in our marriages, in our personal lives, and in our walks with God.

 GETTING ACQUAINTED

A Quick Look at Last Things

Suppose you were to attend your own funeral. You sit in the back row to see those who would attend and to hear what is said about you.

What would you hope to hear from your spouse?

Your children?

Your boss?

Your God?

R.I.P.
If you could capsulize all of those eulogies into one concise statement, what would it be? Fill it in below.

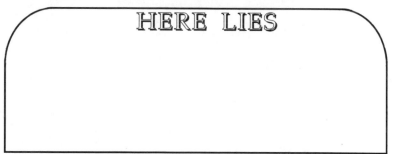

HERE LIES

GAINING INSIGHT

Finishing Well
Our study examines what it means to carry on and hang in there until the end. Our goal is not simply to survive, but to thrive in a life that God has given. The Apostle Paul, enduring prison life, wrote about his desires for his own life. He desired to finish well. And so should we. His helpful insights provide us with strong principles for persevering, even when life is tough.

Read Philippians 3:10–4:1.

[10]I want to know Christ and the power of His resurrection and the fellowship of sharing in His sufferings, becoming like Him in His death, [11]and so, somehow, to attain to the resurrection from the dead.

¹²Not that I have already obtained all this, or have already been made perfect, but I press on to take hold of that for which Christ Jesus took hold of me. ¹³Brothers, I do not consider myself yet to have taken hold of it. But one thing I do: Forgetting what is behind and straining toward what is ahead, ¹⁴I press on toward the goal to win the prize for which God has called me heavenward in Christ Jesus.

¹⁵All of us who are mature should take such a view of things. And if on some point you think differently, that too God will make clear to you. ¹⁶Only let us live up to what we have already attained.

¹⁷Join with others in following my example, brothers, and take note of those who live according to the pattern we gave you. ¹⁸For, as I have often told you before and now say again even with tears, many live as enemies of the cross of Christ. ¹⁹Their destiny is destruction, their god is their stomach, and their glory is in their shame. Their mind is on earthly things. ²⁰But our citizenship is in heaven. And we eagerly await a Savior from there, the Lord Jesus Christ, ²¹who, by the power that enables Him to bring everything under His control, will transform our lowly bodies so that they will be like His glorious body.

¹Therefore, my brothers, you whom I love and long for, my joy and crown, that is how you should stand firm in the Lord, dear friends!

Philippians 3:10–4:1

The beloved apostle may be facing his final days. He may be put to death soon. But that does not matter to him. If he departs and goes to his Lord, this is much better (Philippians 1:22-24). If he stays on earth, this is fine too. Either way, he will rejoice.

Paul's passion for the Lord Jesus is obvious. He wants to live, breathe, and walk a life of devotion. And this is not just for the moment, but for a whole life. A life of absolute, rock solid commitment until the end. He has much to teach us.

Going for the Goal

How would you paraphrase Philippians 3:10 in such a way that would explain the verse to someone who was not familiar with the Scriptures?

What has been Paul's progress in reaching his goal, according to Philippians 3:12-14? What is the focus of Paul's life regarding these goals? To what extent is he willing to go to reach them?

What is the "pattern" to which Paul points in Philippians 3:17?

What difference would following Paul's example make in a marriage?

What kind of enemies might Paul have had in mind when he wrote Philippians 3:18-19?

In what ways do people today show enmity toward the Cross?

How can Christian marriages help form strongholds in a hostile culture?

Paul summarizes this section as an example of how to "stand firm in the Lord" (Philippians 4:1). Look back and note some of the attitudes and actions that make up a firm stance.

How does this translate to present-day living?

What role can spouses play in supporting one another to stand firm?

 ## GROWING BY DOING

Since we are at the end of our eight-session study, let's look back on some of the lessons learned and forward to set some goals for our lives.

Looking Back

Divide up into couples and recall some of the principles that you have remembered from previous sessions. Use the following sentence-starters to guide your discussion, if you wish.

❏ One thing from these sessions that really had an impact on my thinking is . . .

❏ The session or principle that most hit home was . . .

❏ One way I was really challenged was . . .

❑ An area in which I have tried to change my attitudes or actions is . . .

❑ A change I have seen in my marriage is . . .

Looking Ahead
Project some goals for the future in light of the "citizenship in heaven" that Paul mentions.

What can truly be different because of this study?

How do you envision your marriage relationship growing as a result of this study?

Where do you need to go from here to maintain the momentum of what you have learned?

GOING THE SECOND MILE

In My Life
How is your life evidencing "pressing on" to know Christ? To what would you point if someone asked for proof? To what extent do you honestly sense this growth and maturation?

For My Wife or Husband

How will you actively encourage your spouse to live a life of whole-hearted devotion to the Lord Jesus Christ?

For Our Group

Write a prayer for the group that will sum up Paul's desires. Pray this prayer with your spouse.

DEAR SMALL GROUP LEADER:

Picture Yourself As A Leader.

List some words that describe what would excite you or scare you as a leader of your small group.

A Leader Is Not . . .
☐ a person with all the answers.
☐ responsible for everyone having a good time.
☐ someone who does all the talking.
☐ likely to do everything perfectly.

A Leader Is . . .
☐ someone who encourages and enables group members to discover insights and build relationships.
☐ a person who helps others meet their goals, enabling the group to fulfill its purpose.
☐ a protector to keep members from being attacked or taken advantage of.
☐ the person who structures group time and plans ahead.
☐ the facilitator who stimulates relationships and participation by asking questions.
☐ an affirmer, encourager, challenger.

❑ enthusiastic about the small group, about God's Word, and about discovering and growing.

What Is Important To Small Group Members?
❑ A leader who cares about them.
❑ Building relationships with other members.
❑ Seeing themselves grow.
❑ Belonging and having a place in the group.
❑ Feeling safe while being challenged.
❑ Having their reasons for joining a group fulfilled.

What Do You Do . . .

If nobody talks —
❑ Wait — show the group members you expect them to answer.
❑ Rephrase a question — give them time to think.
❑ Divide into subgroups so all participate.

If somebody talks too much —
❑ Avoid eye contact with him or her.
❑ Sit beside the person next time. It will be harder for him or her to talk sitting by the leader.
❑ Suggest, "Let's hear from someone else."
❑ Interrupt with, "Great! Anybody else?"

If people don't know the Bible —
❑ Print out the passage in the same translation and hand it out to save time searching for a passage.
❑ Use the same Bible versions and give page numbers.
❑ Ask enablers to sit next to those who may need encouragement in sharing.
❑ Begin using this book to teach them how to study; affirm their efforts.

If you have a difficult individual —
❑ Take control to protect the group, but recognize that exploring differences can be a learning experience.
❑ Sit next to that person.
❑ To avoid getting sidetracked or to protect another group member, you may need to interrupt, saying, "Not all of us feel that way."
❑ Pray for that person before the group meeting.

ONE

Love is an Action Verb

We've all heard the sayings before the wedding day. "Your freedom ends soon!" "You're finally going to take the plunge." And so we do it, or rather, we say, "I do." Then married bliss begins and lasts until the honeymoon starts! The toughest days of marriage, it is said, are those after the wedding. Some of us find that out right away. Others need to wait a few weeks, months, or even years before the tough times come. But they inevitably come. We recognize that God has given us this other person, but we can't understand why!

On the other hand, some newlyweds soon experience the joy of close companionship, the tender love of two people who are enthralled with each other. It is as if we are walking through an apple orchard in blossom. We can smell the promise of fruitfulness and look forward to even better times. God gave us to each other as partners to share life with. We walk together, eagerly expecting to live life to the full arm in arm, doubling our joy and cutting our sorrows in half. Nothing can stop us now.

Which of the two scenarios describes your first days or months of marriage? Perhaps most are somewhere in between. The pessimist is convinced that things will get worse. The optimist can't wait for tomorrow. The realist sees that we will experience the good with the bad and will just have to make the best of it. The Christian realist understands this as well, but is convinced that God will walk with us through it all.

I believe that when starry-eyed couples take their vows they are absolutely sure that their relationship is the best there ever was and nothing could threaten it. They vow "for better or for worse," but know they will have the best. They say "for richer or for poorer," but see only upward mobility as a possibility. They utter "in sickness and in health," but strength and vitality surely could not fail in their lifetimes. In their idealism they even think that "till death us do part" means they will die on the same day, never to be without each other! When reality hits, the crashing vision creates confusion and chaos in the heart. Slowly the couple can begin to live a life built not on dreamy idealism but on the truth of God's care and provision.

This study is intended to help couples, whatever stage they are in, to move toward greater love, transparency, commitment, and care with a growing faith in God's everlasting love for them and for their marriages.

As **Group Leader** of this small group experience, *you* have a choice as to which elements in each session will best fit your group, your style of leadership, and your purposes. After you examine the **Session Objectives,** select activities under each heading.

SESSION OBJECTIVES

√ To become acquainted and begin to feel at ease in sharing naturally and spontaneously with the group.

√ To relate and apply the Scripture passage to our daily lives.

√ To examine specifically how to make the characteristics linked to full love a part of our experience.

√ To take concrete action on at least one characteristic of love in marriage this week.

√ To pray for one another.

GETTING ACQUAINTED   15–20 minutes

First impressions are lasting impressions. The same is true in group life: First meeting patterns tend to endure. In this study about marriage, it is critical to help couples have good communication patterns. Good communication patterns are just as important for groups. Be sure to give people enough time to think and express themselves.

The **Getting Acquainted** section throughout the book focuses on helping couples to express themselves openly on a relatively nonthreatening basis. These sections also relate to the topic of the session. Time spent here will pay dividends in the group in the form of openness when you ask for reactions to more in-depth questions and thoughts. This section is not to be viewed as "fluff" in preparation for the meat. Consider this a way of whetting the appetite, preparation for proper delivery of weighty truth.

Have a group member read **Weddings and Marriage.** Then choose one or more of the following activities to establish a comfortable atmosphere for your meeting.

Your Wedding
Discussions about a couple's wedding and honeymoon will be both humorous and insightful at times. As people relate their

experiences, they provide a window into family matters and the dynamics of relationships both within their own marriage and within their extended family.

Your Marriage
Use this section as an opportunity to voice dreams, not disappointments. You will also find out what people consider "meaningful." This may give evidence about their own maturity and walk with God.

Pocket Principle

1 Groups thrive when members sense acceptance from one another. It is your job as a leader to encourage an atmosphere of warmth and openness among all. This can be done by discussing the whole issue of acceptance with the group and by modeling acceptance itself. Acceptance is not to be confused with approval. We can accept a person without approving of some of all of that person's behavior.

Love Is . . .
This activity provides a nice transition to the Scripture used in this session.

Optional — Course Overview
Take a few minutes to outline the sessions in this study. Sessions 1 and 2 address the foundations of marriage: love, faith, and commitment. Sessions 3, 4, and 5 help husbands and wives strive toward greater intimacy with each other. The group will explore the topics of communication and the roles we play in marriage and sexuality. Session 6 addresses one area so often associated with marital disharmony: finances. Sessions 7 and 8 help us set our sights on the future. The group will learn and discuss how to lead a balanced life.

GAINING INSIGHT   25–30 minutes

Love in Action
The text under study is 1 Corinthians 13:1-7, 13. You may choose to have someone read the text out loud to help people

focus on the words. While this is a familiar text, we can move beyond the familiarity to the meaning it should have in our lives.

Rewriting verses gives people time to think about the impact of the Scriptures for daily life. While Paul was writing to the Corinthians, who were struggling to act lovingly in the midst of tremendous giftedness, our focus is to bring these important thoughts to bear on marriage. Certainly, this should not be hard. But it does take time to paraphrase a text with meaning. It would be helpful to have several people read what they have written.

My Loving Spouse

This section will both help group members identify qualities they appreciate in their spouses and will offer a glimpse into the personal lives of the group members. You may find that the responses are at first superficial. Given time, people do open up and discuss not only their failings but also their successes.

Optional—More Love, More Action

If you have time, examine some of the other characteristics of love given in this passage. You may wish to invite group members to reflect on how their spouses show these qualities in the same way that you discussed patience, kindness, and lack of boastfulness in **My Loving Spouse.** Or you may prefer to give time for self-evaluation by inviting group members to contrast the prevalence of envy, pride, rudeness, selfishness, and anger in their relationship when they were courting and now.

Pocket Principle

2 For most groups, instant vulnerability and transparency is not possible. Gradual, increasing openness is very "do-able" if we are able to be consistent in providing time for people to talk about their own experiences. Be sure to allow people to volunteer information and not insist they give it.

Partners with Power

The use of our power for the well-being of others is a mark of genuine humility and gentleness. Marriages thrive when each partner is actively making this a priority. Most of the time, however, we don't think about how we use the power tools of speech, money, time, and attitudes. As people recall how they have been beneficially using these on behalf of a spouse, others see how they can effectively do this as well.

GROWING BY DOING   20–25 minutes

I Could Try This

The link between learning and application is thoughtful consideration and brainstorming about how the text of Scripture practically relates to our lives. The strategy to make this happen includes dividing up men and women (who tend to view things differently!) to enhance an atmosphere where ideas can flow. When a man suggests a way he can be more patient and kind with his wife, his suggestion will probably resonate with other men. The same is true with the women. Of course, some ideas will be common to both groups.

Pocket Principle

3 Setting ground rules for communication is vital. Do not allow complaining about a spouse in this session. Our focus is on ourselves and how we can become more like the Lord Jesus in our loving.

I'd Like You to Try That

Sometimes our perceptions of what our spouses would like don't match reality! Give husbands and wives a chance to communicate so that their applications of this Scripture can be truly appropriate to their marriage.

GOING THE SECOND MILE   5 minutes

This section provides opportunities for people to continue the learning and applying process throughout the coming weeks. Group members will benefit most if they can hold one another accountable to accomplish these tasks. Consider setting aside time in the next session to "report" on how these tasks went.

In My Life
The emphasis in this section is personal growth. Encourage group members to set aside time to complete this exercise on their own during the week.

For My Wife or Husband
This section allows us to live out the text in the context of our marriages. The emphasis is usually on action—in this case, love in action. Encourage group members to set aside time to complete this exercise on their own during the week.

For Our Group
Encourage husbands and wives to complete this section together during the week. Pair off couples as "prayer partner couples" for the duration of this study, so that the Joneses pray for the Smiths consistently over the next eight weeks, and the Smiths pray for the Joneses. As we pray for one another, and for the marriages of the group, we pave the way for God's mighty acts to be realized in people's lives.

TWO

Choices

Pulled in so many directions! That is what our world does to us. Sometimes we are drawn to actions and commitments that help our marriages, sometimes not. But we can take charge and build the right foundation for our lives as couples.

Today's session focuses on committing ourselves and our marriages to serve the Lord.

As **Group Leader** of this small group experience, *you* have a choice as to which elements in each session will best fit your group, your style of leadership, and your purposes. After you examine the **Session Objectives,** select activities under each heading.

SESSION OBJECTIVES

√ To recognize God's faithfulness in our lives.

√ To respond to God's faithfulness with a new or renewed commitment to serve Him.

√ To discover concrete ways to serve God in our marriages.

√ To identify the lures and dangers of modern idolatry.

GETTING ACQUAINTED   15–20 minutes

Have a group member read **Hype or Hope?** Then choose one or more of the following activities to establish a comfortable atmosphere for your meeting.

Learning the Trail from Trailblazers

People who have given us sound advice are worth holding in high regard. We have been blessed by their counsel. Chances are, others would also be helped by the same words. This time of hearing from others is helpful in knitting the group together.

Trail Map

Group members do not need to have artistic ability to complete this activity. Use this as a nonthreatening way to share a little about members' personal experiences of marriage.

Optional — Accountability Sharing

Spend some time in groups of three or four sharing how people were able to fulfill last week's **Going the Second Mile** section. Encourage an atmosphere of affirming accountability; this is not a time for guilt trips.

GAINING INSIGHT   30–35 minutes

Looking Back

Invite one or more volunteers to read the Scripture passage.

Pocket Principle

1 Many people have a difficult time reading, especially out loud before others. They feel very self-conscious and inadequate. It is not wise to "read around the circle" unless you know for certain that this is agreeable to all. You might be surprised at how terrified some are at the thought of reading in front of others. Ask for volunteers instead.

As you discuss the Scripture sections, use the following information to supplement group responses:

☐ Joshua 24:2-4: The focus here is on the covenant given to Abraham. The Jews looked to Abraham as their father. His place in their heritage is deeply treasured. Joshua reminds the people that the God of Abraham is their own God. He is a covenant-making and -keeping God.

☐ Joshua 24:5-7: The Exodus experience is still recounted as God's mighty delivering act in the life of Israel. Joshua reminds the people that God is certainly powerful enough to deliver them now.

☐ Joshua 24:11-13: Each of the conquests of the Israelites was not due to their own might, but to God's might. God is the Almighty One.

Allow ample time for group members to share their own experiences of God's faithfulness.

Time to Choose
Ask volunteers to share their responses to the questions in this section.

Pocket Principle

2 Occasionally group members will be asked to note something specific from a Scripture passage, like the three commands in this section. While this exercise is helpful for focusing on what is important in the passage, it is not helpful as a discussion question. Avoid discussing questions with obvious or "right" answers and instead focus on application and personal experience questions.

As you discuss contemporary "idolatry," note that we face many temptations to replace God as the focus of life. Even our relationships may become false gods to us. Family is important, but it must not be allowed to reign supreme. Christian devotion and service are vital elements in life. Our family members need to see that even our relationships with them are secondary to a relationship with God.

GROWING BY DOING 15–20 minutes

As for Me . . .
Invite volunteers to share their faith journeys, but be sensitive to those who may not be certain of their commitment. Make time to be available to anyone who would like to talk privately about committing his or her life to God.

Pocket Principle

3 Testimonies can be greatly inspiring to the hearers. Regular people telling how they have focused on God encourages all. Hearing how God is on the throne of our lives builds everyone up. Take time to hear about others' spiritual journeys with the Lord.

And My Household
We often are busy, but at times we intentionally choose busyness to cover and conceal a heart far away from God. We choose not to serve God but these activities. After the groups of two or three couples have discussed the questions in this section, invite them to share their most helpful suggestions.

GOING THE SECOND MILE 5 minutes

In My Life
Encourage people to take a sincere look this week at where they are in their relationship with God. Ask them to think

seriously about what they can do to improve this.

For My Wife or Husband
Trying to be encouraging spiritually to a spouse is tricky business. This is where listening to what they want is the best method. Encourage people to listen intently before they plan.

For Our Group
Encourage couples to think of ways to offer concrete support this week. What about offering to baby-sit the kids for a couple who are both involved in leading the youth group? Or bringing a meal on meeting night to lighten the load for active committee members? Urge couples to think of support they can offer *together;* if one spouse ends up doing all the work, the marriage will probably not be enhanced!

THREE

Can We Talk?

True communication is not merely talking. But what we say and how we say it is certainly a big part of communication. The Scriptures give us valuable insight on how to rightly and respectfully use our tongues for maximum benefit. This should be the focus of our time talking: to build up, not destroy. So, when asked, "Can we talk?" the answer is a hearty, "Yes!" But we will talk God's way.

As **Group Leader** of this small group experience, *you* have a choice as to which elements in each session will best fit your group, your style of leadership, and your purposes. After you examine the **Session Objectives,** select activities under each heading.

SESSION OBJECTIVES

√ To identify problem areas in communication that pose barriers to true understanding.

√ To explore healthy ways of dealing with anger in relationships.

√ To commit to concrete expressions of kindness and compassion in our marriages.

GETTING ACQUAINTED   15–20 minutes

Have a group member read **Sticks and Stones May Break My Bones. . . .** Then choose one or more of the following activities to establish a comfortable atmosphere for your meeting.

Road Warriors

Whether we like to admit it or not, how we respond on the road is a pretty good indication of our attitudes, if not our actions, toward those who "cut us off" in other areas of life.

Old and New

Use these questions to learn a little more about one another, as well as to move from sharing nonthreatening memories to more personal openness about spiritual experiences.

Optional—Accountability Sharing

Spend some time in groups of three or four sharing how people were able to fulfill last week's **Going the Second Mile** section.

GAINING INSIGHT   30–35 minutes

Putting Off the Old

The first three chapters of Ephesians provide a rather detailed description of how God has provided the richness of His grace for the church. He opened the door to a relationship with the living God through the death and resurrection of Christ. Such a privilege is not without responsibilities, however. In chapters four through six, Paul delineates those responsibilities. We must act as a new people of God who are not inclined to live with ungodly patterns. We are to act with new life even in our everyday, mundane situations—even in our marriages.

Discuss the following questions in this section:

❑ **Paul speaks of putting off the old self with all of the destructive behaviors that go along with our old way of life. As you think about your communication patterns, what are the words and behaviors that could** tend to "shut down" true, open, honest communication? Can you think of any examples of how they might appear in marriages? (Talking "in theory" about barriers in communication in marriage is safe. Couples need not reveal that they themselves are have these barriers, only that they are possible. This "primes the pump" for owning some of these shortcomings as our own.)

❏ Why do we tend to get locked in such patterns when we know they are not helpful? (Often we repeat the patterns we've seen in our parents' marriages. Or we react in unhealthy patterns because we feel attacked and want to hurt the other person.)

❏ Which of these do you see in your own communication style? Do you, personally, have any tendencies in this area? (Try to keep people looking at themselves and their own patterns, not their spouses' patterns. A person can only confess his or her own sins, not a spouse's. Similarly, a person can only change himself or herself.)

Pocket Principle

1 Remember that you do not have to solve all the communication problems in the group. Feel free to suggest to people that trained counselors may be the most effective way to handle specific problems.

Speech Class
Identify the twin commands of Ephesians 4:25, then discuss the questions in the rest of the section.

At the end of the section, list the admonitions in Ephesians 4:32, but save discussion of them for the **Growing by Doing** section.

GROWING BY DOING   15–20 minutes

Kind and Compassionate
It is helpful if you can divide the group by gender for this discussion. Men can help other men plan kind and compas-

sionate acts for their wives and vice versa. This kind of brain-storming can also help to further open up discussion about the needs represented within the group.

GOING THE SECOND MILE   5 minutes

In My Life
Encourage group members to give serious consideration to the issues in this section. There may be considerable pain in some couples' lives.

For My Wife or Husband
This can be a fun and fruitful way to open or enhance communication during the week.

For Our Group
The principles in Ephesians 4 apply to relationships within the group as well as within marriage. Encourage couples to think of simple ways to show kindness or compassion. Perhaps some of the ideas they listed in the **Growing by Doing** section would be appropriate for other couples as well as for spouses.

FOUR

Recipe for Maximum Enjoyment

We all want fulfillment in this era. We desire it in our jobs, in our personal lives, in our relationship with God, and in our marriages. Many times this means that we neglect others in our pursuit of happiness. This ought not to be. With some helpful admonitions from the Apostle Paul, we can begin to focus on what true fulfillment is, not on what our world says it should be. And in so doing, as we search for true fulfillment God's way, we can then truly live in maximum enjoyment.

As **Group Leader** of this small group experience, *you* have a choice as to which elements in each session will best fit your group, your style of leadership, and your purposes. After you examine the **Session Objectives,** select activities under each heading.

SESSION OBJECTIVES

√ To look at the commands and roles of marriage in the light of being filled by the Spirit of God.
√ To identify practical ways to submit to one another.
√ To develop an attitude of gratitude for one another in marriage.

GETTING ACQUAINTED   15–20 minutes

Have a group member read **Half-baked or Heavenly?** Then choose one or more of the following activities to establish a comfortable atmosphere for your meeting.

Just Desserts

Sometimes we ask questions of others that seem to be inconsequential, but they actually do bear fruit. Since we are dealing with the idea of following a recipe for maximum marriage enjoyment, it is reasonable to think about food. And so we ask people about their favorite dessert and why they like it. People will "connect" with each other as they agree with one another and spur one another on with delicious ideas.

Choice Ingredients

We move to the idea of considering who may be a model of an honorable marriage in order to think about the "ingredients" of what makes marriage work well. This provides us an easy entry into the Bible study portion of the meeting, where we consider Paul's ideas for living rightly in relationships.

Optional—Accountability Sharing

Spend some time in groups of three or four sharing how people were able to fulfill last week's **Going the Second Mile** section.

GAINING INSIGHT   20–25 minutes

Living Wisely

Invite one or more volunteers to read the Scripture passage.

General Guidelines

It is very important to consider a biblical statement made in the context of the overall paragraph, chapter, and book. This is especially true in our current study of Ephesians 5:15-33. Many would jump immediately to Ephesians 5:22 and begin to make rules about how wives should act in the marriage relationship. Isolating one verse or a collection of verses is one way to miss the meaning. The overall discussion about how to live in relationships in general serves as a backdrop to the issues about husband-wife, child-parent, and slave-master relationships Paul discusses.

So we turn to the couplets Paul gives in 5:15, 17, 18. Paul urges (1) that we live as wise people, (2) that we understand God's will, and (3) that we become filled by the Spirit. These are not to be passed over lightly. You may wish to ask people to consider an area whcre they are not living wisely and then to turn from it. Perhaps it would be helpful to talk about what "wise living" looks like.

Spirit-filled living is another concept worth pondering. Fortunately Paul tells us what this looks like. He lists these behaviors in 5:19-21. They are:

- ❏ speaking to one another in psalms, hymns, and spiritual songs;
- ❏ singing and making music in your heart to God;
- ❏ giving thanks for everything;
- ❏ submitting to one another out of reverence for Christ.

Spend time discussing how we can live out these guidelines in contemporary society.

Guidelines for Marriage
It is very important that people understand that the specifics of verses 22-33 are an outgrowth of a couple's adherence to the principles of Spirit-filled living. When we talk about submission of wife to husband and the giving of husband for wife, we are doing so with the realization that both are to be exhibiting a life controlled by the Spirit of God.

When it comes to the command of mutually submitting, each should take responsibility for himself or herself. It is not right to order someone to submit. The manner of Jesus, which is cited as the example for the husband, entails of giving all for the wife. Total, selfless giving for a wife maintains an atmosphere for enjoyment for both.

It could be interesting to divide into same-sex groups to discuss what voluntary submission and its abuse might look like today. Then have the women and the men share their conclusions and discuss any differences in perspective.

GROWING BY DOING   25–30 minutes

Submission Scenarios

Encourage group members to describe realistic conflicts, but also encourage them to refrain from listing personal details from their own marital conflicts that could be hurtful to their spouses.

Pocket Principle

1 When doing role plays, don't be afraid to stop the action to discuss what is going on, or to cut a role play short if the actors do not seem to be resolving the conflict. Focus as much on process and attitudes as on final solutions.

The Spirit-filled Marriage

Discussing the topic of spiritual fullness and working toward it are two different things. People may be very willing to talk about it and consider it on the intellectual level, but actually taking steps to apply the principles is a matter of the will and heart, as well as the mind. You, as the leader, can model this through sharing your own goals and decisions.

GOING THE SECOND MILE   5 minutes

In My Life

Challenge group members to complete this section on their own.

For My Wife or Husband

You may need to give testimony to your own experience of the value of praying together as a couple to give the idea a gentle "push." Ask couples to report back on their progress.

Pocket Principle

2 The value of personal testimony in a group setting is immense. Rather than the leader always speaking about his or her own experience, ask another member of the group to speak and describe the blessings and encouragement that come

from a Spirit-directed life or a life of prayer with a spouse.

For Our Group

Let group members know that no one will be forced to share this statement, and that those who are willing to share next week will do so in groups of three or four. Smaller groups can be less intimidating than sharing with the whole group.

FIVE

One Plus One Equals One

Talk about sex? Why not! Our whole society is talking about it, so it only makes sense that we bring God's view to bear on the contemporary scene. Sex is a special gift to aid intimacy. We can look at it squarely and discern how it can be most fulfilling.

Sexual intimacy without the covenant of marriage and the intimacy that results from it is perversion. It is also true that marriage, with the intimacy that should attend it, is an aberration without the physical expression of love. While it is possible, sometimes even necessary, to have a temporary lack of physical expression in marriage, the sexual relationship between husband and wife is to be part of a growing marriage. So, to this topic we turn as part of a full series on making the marriage bond stronger.

As **Group Leader** of this small group experience, *you* have a choice as to which elements in each session will best fit your group, your style of leadership, and your purposes. After you examine the **Session Objectives,** select activities under each heading.

SESSION OBJECTIVES

√ To examine biblical teachings about sexual expression, both the importance of it for marriage and the danger of it being expressed outside of marriage.

√ To look at the way society tempts us to act dishonorably in the sexual area.

√ To identify ways to support one another in sexual purity.

√ To talk openly with our spouses about the sexual relationship.

 ## GETTING ACQUAINTED   15–20 minutes

Before you address this session's topic, make time to share in groups of three or four the statements that group members wrote as part of last session's **Going the Second Mile.** Then have a group member read **Strange Mathematics.** Choose one or more of the following activities to establish a comfortable atmosphere for your meeting.

A Great Idea!
Sexual expression of love does not stand on its own. It is inextricably connected to a vital relationship. One aspect of adding spice to an otherwise "regular" relationship is romance. Romance lights a fire of love that can glow in marriage. Perhaps it would be helpful for couples to talk separately and then come together as a group. Ideas will generate more ideas for your couples.

Sex and Romance
In this section, couples may find that they share a perspective—or they may learn something about each other they didn't know!

 ## GAINING INSIGHT   30–35 minutes

Sex for Christians
Ask volunteers to read the introductory paragraph and the Scripture.

Sex outside Marriage

Paul addresses two sides of human sexuality. First he deals with improper sexual behaviors.

Discuss these questions.

❑ **Based on this passage, how would you respond to a person who says, "I feel that my sexual behavior has nothing to do with my religion, because sex is physical and religion is spiritual"?** (This passage focuses on the idea of connection. A vital connection takes place in the sexual act. This connecting reaches the deepest part of our being. Here Paul uses the same word, "unite," to describe the sexual union and the union between Christ and the believer. While one union is in the realm of the body and the other the spirit, both are union nonetheless.)

❑ **Do you think that this passage demonstrates that sexual sin is worse than other kinds of sin? Why or why not?** (It can be helpful to think of two results of sin: guilt and damage. All sin is offense against God, so all sins make us equally guilty. But some sins cause greater damage than others. While this passage does not give those who have not fallen into sexual sin the right to look down on those who have, it would be unrealistic not to admit that the damage—both to self and others—resulting from sexual sin is usually greater than the damage resulting from, say, taking home office supplies for personal use.)

❑ **How does the fact that you were bought at a price (6:20) motivate you?** (The believer has been bought with the price of the death of the Son of God. This should guarantee not only our allegiance to God, but also our honoring God in our bodies as well as our spirits. Invite participants to share their personal responses to this great sacrifice.)

Sex within Marriage

Paul moves from discussing immoral behavior to sexual expression within marriage.

Discuss the following questions.

102

❑ **Sex as a duty (7:3) is not a popular concept. In what ways do husbands and wives have responsibilities to each other sexually? What are the benefits to the spouse of fulfilling those responsibilities? What are the benefits to the marriage?** (Marriage can provide a haven of godly sexual expression for two believers of the opposite sex. And this is ordained of God. It is certainly the responsibility of each in the marriage bond to be concerned about fulfilling the other's sexual needs and desires.)

❑ **What obstacles might prevent couples from fulfilling their responsibilities to each other?** (Many practical obstacles, like exhaustion or lack of time, prevent busy couples from making a priority of sexual intimacy. You will have a chance to explore these obstacles more fully in the **Growing by Doing** section. Sometimes a cessation of sexual intercourse is unavoidable—during severe sickness or immediately after childbirth, for example. But it is not right for there to be a continual withholding of sex, even for spiritual reasons. Deep-seated problems of resentment or selfishness in a relationship can also interfere with sexual expression in marriage.)

Pocket Principle

1 Never force anyone to share. Especially when dealing with potentially sensitive topics, emphasize that no one is required to talk. Only those who wish to speak need to speak.

❑ **How do you feel about your body not belonging to you alone? (7:4)** (Allow for personal responses. Acknowledge and accept that this perspective can make people feel vulnerable.)

❑ **How does this perspective run counter to society's attitudes?** (Our culture takes pains to contradict this perspective, particularly with respect to women—in part in reaction to abuse. The entire pro-choice movement is based on the premise that a woman's body is her own to do with what she chooses.)

❑ **How might the idea of a person's body belonging to his or her spouse be abused?** (Certainly spousal abuse falls into this category. So do other less dramatic abuses, such as selfish insistence on sex when and how one partner wants it, regardless of the other's wishes.)

❑ **How could the idea be honored in a way that is truly pleasing to God and to the spouse?** (When partners in a marriage are as concerned for the other as for themselves, the giving of their bodies in physical intimacy can indeed break down distinctions of "ownership," resulting instead in being "one flesh.")

❑ **Paul suggests that sexual intimacy in marriage is a defense against temptation (7:5). In what ways is this the case?** (Note that we are talking about two words: sexual intimacy. Sex is the motivation for many men to enter extramarital affairs. When physical desires are satisfied at home, men are less tempted to look outside the marriage for sex. But the desire for intimacy, not sex, is what prompts most women to enter affairs. So sex must move beyond the physical act and become an expression of intimacy to fulfill needs in the marriage.)

GROWING BY DOING   15–20 minutes

Supporting One Another
Because of the nature of our society, frank discussion about sexual temptation in general drives one to consider how vulnerable we are. It may be appropriate to separate men and women at this point since the forms of sexual temptation and lures to immorality tend to be different depending on gender.

Who's Got the Time/Energy/Privacy . . . ?
Take some time to talk about some of the practical, if mundane, obstacles to a fulfilling sex life. Set as a ground rule that no personal criticisms or complaints of spouses are permitted. Rather, use this time to identify external difficulties like too much work to get done at home, lack of energy, a need to unwind after the kids are in bed, and so on. Be sure to let the groups listen to each other and then brainstorm ways to alleviate their spouses' stresses.

Pocket Principle

2 Sharing personal experiences and concerns helps a group bond together. But sharing things that might embarrass or reflect badly on another person is inappropriate. Remind group members of this ground rule whenever a discussion might provide the opportunity for invading another's privacy.

GOING THE SECOND MILE   5 minutes

In My Life
Assure group members that these very private reflections will remain private. No one will be asked to share what he or she has written.

For My Wife or Husband
You may wish to tell the group that you will ask about their romantic dates at the next meeting.

For Our Group
Perhaps you might ask some volunteers to read the prayers they wrote during the next meeting.

SIX

Money — Yours, Mine, and Ours

Money is the root of all conflict in marriage. An overstatement? Probably. Money is not the root of all evil, as some people say (misquoting the Bible). But the topic of money is surely one of the sore spots in many of today's marriages. The problem, often, is not mismanagement, but a mistaken orientation toward money and a misunderstanding of whose it is.

As **Group Leader** of this small group experience, *you* have a choice as to which elements in each session will best fit your group, your style of leadership, and your purposes. After you examine the **Session Objectives,** select activities under each heading.

SESSION OBJECTIVES

√ To identify practical strategies for guarding against greed.

√ To assess what we really value in our lives and in our marriages.

√ To reflect on God's care as an antidote to worry.

GETTING ACQUAINTED   15–20 minutes

Have a group member read **Budget Blues.** Then choose one
or more of the following activities to establish a comfortable
atmosphere for your meeting.

Your First Purchase
Remembering your first major purchase provides an insight
into what you considered important early on in life. These
tidbits provide people a window to who you are. Most people
would probably find that those early purchases do not have a
role in their lives currently. But they may have interests
presently that are along the same lines. Even our current
possessions show us what we consider important.

Optional – Accountability Sharing
Spend some time in groups of three or four sharing statements written for last week's **Going the Second Mile** section.

GAINING INSIGHT   30–35 minutes

True Treasure
Invite volunteers to read aloud the paragraphs and Scripture
in this section.

Summarize the two main segments of the Scripture.

❑ **Luke 12:13-21** (First of all Jesus is asked about an inheritance that a younger brother wished to receive from an
   older brother. It was not uncommon for an inheritance to
   be given to an elder brother, who would then distribute
   the amount to other heirs. While the older brother received more, the younger brother also would receive
   something. It is also possible that the inheritance was in
   the form of property that would need to be sold before it
   could be divided among the heirs. The elder brother
   would hold "veto power" over such a decision and could
   prevent the division of assets. Either way, Jesus is urged
   to force the older brother into distributing the wealth.
   Jesus refuses and uses the occasion to teach on greed. He
   tells a parable to warn the disciples of the folly of a life

107

focused on the acquisition of things. It is very presumptuous to think that we will have a future of simply enjoying what we have earned. We must be rich toward God, not rich in possessions.)

☐ **Luke 12:22-34** (Jesus teaches about the folly of worry. If we truly are more important than birds to God, then can't we trust Him to care for us? Worrying accomplishes nothing. In addition, while the pagan world runs after possessions and necessities of life, the heavenly Father knows what we, His children, need. Since we do not have to expend needless emotional and mental energy worrying, let us seek God's Kingdom. Where our treasure is, there will our heart also be. So where will we invest?)

Rich Fools
As you discuss this section, focus especially on the following questions and how they apply within marriage:

☐ **Practically speaking, how does one guard against greed?**
☐ **If a man's (or woman's) life "does not consist in the abundance of his possessions" (v. 15), of what does it consist? On what do you place value?**

Why Worry? Discuss the four questions as a whole group. After discussing the final question, you may wish to break into couples so each couple can discuss practical applications for their own marriage.

GROWING BY DOING   15–20 minutes

Tough Truth
Time spent in this section will be well worth the effort. Much fruit will be gained in discussion.

Pocket Principle

1 To involve everyone in the discussion when you have several statements for the group to react to, break into smaller groups and have each group address

only one Issue. Then the groups can come together to share their findings.

GOING THE SECOND MILE   5 minutes

In My Life
Attitudes and decisions go hand in hand. People will realize that in their lives they may be lacking both the right thoughts and actions. This section will hopefully bring feet to faith.

For My Wife or Husband
Encourage couples to talk over this section together.

For Our Group
Plan to make time for group members to share next week.

SEVEN

Living a Life Daily

Life is so daily! It keeps coming at us. If we are not careful, weeks and months pass by without our taking the time to work on our key relationships. But God gives us advice for thriving even during the mundane times of life. This session's focus is on God's expectations and provisions for us in the daily grind.

As **Group Leader** of this small group experience, *you* have a choice as to which elements in each session will best fit your group, your style of leadership, and your purposes. After you examine the **Session Objectives,** select activities under each heading.

SESSION OBJECTIVES

√ To identify strategies for restoring one another to fellowship after sin.

√ To experience sharing and helping carry one another's burdens.

√ To commit to "sowing" to please the Spirit.

GETTING ACQUAINTED   10–15 minutes

Have a group member read **Same Old Same Old.** Then choose one or more of the following activities to establish a comfortable atmosphere for your meeting.

A Daily Life
Our text, Galatians 6:1-10, contains the injunction to bear one another's burdens. But that is possible only when we know what those burdens are. By this time in your group you have become much better acquainted with your fellow group members. As members talk about their lives, they can open up and share the tough things that drag them down in life.

Divide into groups of four to discuss the questions in this section. The initial activity of listing a typical day's routine may reveal that some group members (notably those at home with small children) have no "typical" day and virtually no routine! Verbally recognize this as a challenge these group members face, not as a failing! Carpooling and changing diapers is just as much a grind as leading board meetings.

Optional—Accountability Sharing
Spend some time in groups of three or four sharing how people were able to fulfill last week's **Going the Second Mile** section.

GAINING INSIGHT   20–25 minutes

More Than a Grind
The section under study, Galatians 6:1-10, is divided very nicely into three parts. The first of these concerns how we handle personal sin while being in relationship with others. The second concerns our responsibility for helping when help is needed—but not helping when someone should be self-sufficient. The final part addresses where we should put our efforts in our lives.

Ask volunteers to read the introductory paragraph and the Scripture.

Concerning Sinning

Galatians 6:1 provides us with a viewpoint on sin. Restoration of the sinner is of utmost importance. The sinner may not always greet us with joy and a willingness to be restored. But that should not dissuade us from attempting to have a positive, correcting role in another's life. Yet we are not immune to temptation ourselves, and we must be on our guard.

Concerning Sharing

Helping others in need does not mean we are superior. This is what Paul is getting at in Galatians 6:2-5. Being helpful does not give us the right to rule or become haughty. We certainly should consider what we do as important, but we should not compare ourselves with others. Paul gives us a picture that a big load (the meaning of the word "burden" in 6:2) ought to be shared, but a smaller load that is capable of being handled by a single person (the meaning of the word "load" in 6:5) ought to be handled alone. The bigger loads we must share with one another.

Pocket Principle

1 When "burdens" are shared, it is appropriate to stop the "study" portion of the meeting and pray, depending on the leading of the Holy Spirit. Don't be afraid to throw out the agenda if overwhelming needs require great prayer.

Concerning Sowing

In the final section, Paul urges us to be involved in doing good. These good deeds will provide a harvest for us in the life to come. Notice that good is to be done for all, with a particular emphasis on those within the Kingdom of God.

 GROWING BY DOING   30–35 minutes

Bearing One Another's Burdens

Have each couple complete this section with the prayer partner couple they were assigned in session 1—the same couple they have been praying for in the **For Our Group** section of **Going the Second Mile.** If your couples have not formed

112

prayer partners during this study, simply form groups of four for this exercise.

This section is a prayer request ledger. Encourage group members to write down other people's concerns. Then follow through by asking for prayer volunteers and active helpers if the situation presents itself to the group.

 ## GOING THE SECOND MILE 5 minutes

In My Life
Challenge group members to complete this section on their own.

For My Wife or Husband
Urge group members to actively share their spouses' burdens. Ask for reports during the next meeting to see what actions have resulted.

For Our Group
Challenge group members to complete this section on their spouses.

EIGHT

Strength Enough to Finish

Hanging in there for the long haul is a constant concern in marriage. We all know of times when we have taken this relationship for granted and slipped into poor habits. It takes work to advance in intimacy. In this session we focus on the importance of finishing well.

As **Group Leader** of this small group experience, *you* have a choice as to which elements in each session will best fit your group, your style of leadership, and your purposes. After you examine the **Session Objectives,** select activities under each heading.

SESSION OBJECTIVES

√ To put into words the qualities we would like to be remembered for.

√ To examine the goal that Paul was striving for as an example for us.

√ To reflect on what we have learned and how we have grown in this eight-session study.

√ To make spiritual growth a goal to focus on in our marriages.

GETTING ACQUAINTED   15–20 minutes

Have a group member read **Secrets to Success.** Then choose one or more of the following activities to establish a comfortable atmosphere for your meeting.

A Quick Look at Last Things

Many times looking at the end helps one at the beginning. Knowing what our target looks like certainly helps us to hit it! What do group members want to be remembered for at the end of their lives? This is sobering, perhaps even a bit morbid. But it gets us to focus on what matters and is truly important. This look at "last things" also can help determine next steps.

R.I.P.

To help group members consolidate their goals and reflect on what is really important, have them capsulize their desired epitaph in one statement.

Optional—Accountability Sharing

Spend some time in groups of three or four sharing how people were able to fulfill last week's **Going the Second Mile** section.

GAINING INSIGHT   30–45 minutes

Finishing Well

Invite volunteers to read this section aloud.

Going for the Goal

Paul's goal was to know Christ and the power of the resurrection and the fellowship of the sufferings of Christ. Paul indeed knew what it was to minister in the power of the Spirit of God. He lived a life of suffering for the sake of the Gospel. He desired to be with Christ above all else. His pattern is worth emulating. We need to consider seriously what it means to live this way. And this life of devotion should extend to a marriage. We must live for the long term.

115

As you discuss this section, focus especially on the following questions, which apply the Scripture particularly to marriage:

❑ **What difference would following Paul's example make in a marriage?**
❑ **How can Christian marriages help form strongholds in a hostile culture?**
❑ **What role can spouses play in supporting one another to stand firm?**

GROWING BY DOING   15–20 minutes

Looking Back
You may wish to divide into smaller groups to consider how the overall series has helped couples. Then it would be absolutely appropriate to ask couples to take time to pray with one another about these things. Perhaps you could take time for testimonies and celebrate what God has done in your midst.

Pocket Principle

1 A sense of closure is vital to a good group experience. Reminding ourselves and one another of what we have learned helps bring the study to conclusion and affirms the value of our time together.

Looking Ahead
Encourage one another to not consider yourselves graduates or experts on marriage now, but to continue "pressing on."

GOING THE SECOND MILE   5 minutes

In My Life
Challenge group members to complete this section on their own.

For My Wife or Husband
Challenge group members to complete this section on their own.

For Our Group
As you reflect on the needs and benefits of your group, pray for the group with your spouse. As leaders, you can model this activity in your group. Then encourage the group to do this on their own.